WAY-COOL

FRENCH
Phrase Book

PASSPORT BOOKS

About this book

Jane Wightwick
had the idea

Wina Gunn
wrote the pages

Leila Gaafar (aged 10)
drew the first pictures in
each chapter

Robert Bowers
(not aged 10) drew the
other pictures, and
designed the book

Marie–Claude Dunleavy
did the French stuff

Important things that **must** be included

First published in the United States in 2001 by

Passport Books
A division of The McGraw-Hill Companies.
4255 West Touhy Avenue, Lincolnwood (Chicago),
Illinois 60712-1975 U.S.A.

Printed in Singapore

Library of Congress Catalog Card Number: **00-135716**

International Standard Book Number: 0-658-01690-3

01 02 03 04 05   15 14 13 12 11 10 9 8 7 6 5 4 3 2

What's inside

Making friends

How to be cool with the group

Wanna play?

Our guide to joining in everything from hide-and-seek to the latest electronic game

Feeling hungry

Order your favorite foods or go local

Looking good

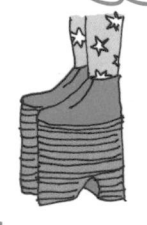

Make sure you keep up with all those essential fashions

Hanging out

At the pool, beach, or theme park—don't miss out on the action

Pocket money

Spend it here!

Grown-up talk

blah! blah! blah! blah!

If you really, really have to!

Extra stuff

All the handy things—numbers, months, time, days of the week

MAKING FRIENDS

me
moi 👄 mwa

my snake
mon serpent
👄 mo sir-pon

my friend
mon copain
👄 mo ko-pa

my friend
ma copine
👄 ma ko-pee

my dog
mon chien
👄 mo shee-a

my big brother
mon grand frère
👄 mo gro frair

dad
papa
👄 pah-pah

grandpa
papi
👄 pah-pee

grandma
mamie
👄 ma-mee

mom
maman
👄 ma-mon

my little sister
ma petite sœur
👄 ma pteet sir

Half a step this way

stepfather/stepmother
beau-père/belle-mère
👄 bow pair/bel mair

stepbrother/ stepsister
beau-frère/ belle-sœur
👄 bow frair/bel sir

half brother/half sister
demi frère/demi sœur
👄 demee frair/demee sir

MAKING FRIENDS

7

Hi!
Salut!
👄 saloo

What's your name?
Comment tu t'appelles?
👄 ko-mo too tapel

My name's ...
Je m'appelle ...
👄 jer mapel

Are you OK?
Ça va?
👄 sa va

Cool, and you?
Ça boom, et toi?
👄 sa boom, eh twa

Kissing is extremely popular among French children. You can't possibly say hello to your friends in the morning without kissing them on both cheeks. Try this in front of your mirror if your friends at home won't let you experiment on them.

Where are you from?
T'es d'où?
👄 tay doo?

from Canada
de Canada
👄 day kana-da

from Ireland
d'Irelande
👄 deer-lond

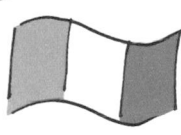

from Scotland
d'Écosse
👄 day-cos

from Wales
du Pays de Galles
👄 doo pay-ee der gal

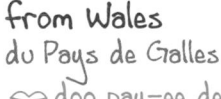

from the U.S.
des États Unis
👄 days etaz-oo-nee

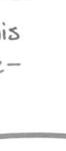

from England
d'Angleterre
👄 donglutair

9

How old are you?
T'as quel âge?
👄 ta kel azh

12 years old
Douze ans
👄 dooz on

Happy birthday!
Bon anniversaire!
👄 bon anee-versair

What's your star sign?
C'est quoi, ton signe astrologique?
👄 say kwa toh seen-yastrolojeek

When's your birthday?
C'est quand, ton anniversaire?
👄 say kon, ton anee-versair

French children often sing "Happy Birthday" in English when the candles are blown out on the cake. So you can practice singing the words with a French accent!

appee birzday too yoo!
appee birzday too yoo!

Star Signs

AQUARIUS
Jan. 21 – Feb. 19
le Verseau ∽ ler ver–so

PISCES
Feb. 20 – Mar. 20
les Poissons ∽ lay pwason

ARIES
Mar. 21 – Apr. 20
le Bélier ∽ ler belly–er

TAURUS
Apr. 21 – May 21
le Taureau ∽ ler tor–oh

GEMINI
May 22 – June 21
les Gémeaux ∽ lay Jem–oh

CANCER
June 22 – July 23
le Cancer ∽ ler cancer

LEO
July 24 – Aug. 23
le Lion ∽ ler lee–on

VIRGO
Aug. 24 – Sep. 23
la Vierge ∽ la vee–erj

LIBRA
Sep. 24 – Oct. 23
la Balance ∽ la ba–lons

SCORPIO
Oct. 24 – Nov.22
le Scorpion ∽ ler scorpion

SAGITTARIUS
Nov. 23 – Dec. 21
le Sagittaire ∽ ler sajitair

CAPRICORN
Dec. 22 – Jan. 20
le Capricorne ∽ ler capricorn

12

soccer
le foot
👄 ler foot

rollerskating/ rollerblading
le roller
👄 ler roller

music
la musique
👄 la mew-zeek

electronic games
les jeux électroniques
👄 lay jer ay-lek-tro-neek

tv
la télé
👄 la taylay

comics
la BD
👄 la bay-day

teddy bears
les nounours
👄 lay noonoor

school
l'école
👄 lay-kol

spiders
les araignées
👄 layz aran-nyay

13

What's your favorite ...?
Quel est ton/ta ... préféré(e)?
🗣 kel ay ton/tah ... preh-fairay

group
(ton) groupe
🗣 (ton) groop

color
(ta) couleur
🗣 (tah) koo-ler

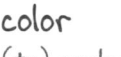

Page 51

food
(ton) plat
🗣 (ton) pla

team
(ton) équipe
🗣 (ton) ekeep

animal
(ton) animal
🗣 (ton) a-nee-mal

dog
le chien
ler shee–an

cat
le chat
ler sha

guinea pig
le cobaye
ler kor-bay

snake
le serpent
ler sir-pon

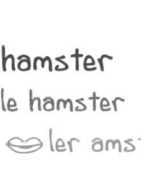

hamster
le hamster
ler amster

parakeet
la perruche
la peroosh

My little doggy goes *oua-oua-oua!*

A French doggy (that's "toutou" in baby language) doesn't say "woof, woof," it says *"oua, oua"* (*waa-waa*). A French sheep says *"bêê, bêê!"* (*bear-bear*) and a cluck-cluck in French chicken-speak is *"cot-cot"* (*ko-ko*). But a cat does say *"miaow"* and a cow *"moo"* whether they're speaking French or English!

Talk about school (if you can stand it)

geography
la géo
🗨 la jay-o

PE
la gym
🗨 la jeem

art
le dessin
🗨 ler dessa

French
le français
🗨 ler fron-say

math
les maths
🗨 lay mat

English
l'anglais
🗨 lon-glay

music
la musique
🗨 la mew-zeek

science
les sciences
👄 lay see-yons

history
l'histoire
👄 lis-twar

Way unfair!

French children have very long vacation breaks: 9 weeks in the summer and another 6–7 weeks throughout the rest of the year. But before you turn green with envy, you might not like the mounds of "**devoirs de vacances**" (*der-vwa der vacans*), that's "vacation homework!" And if you fail your exams, the teachers could make you repeat the whole year with your little sister!

Gossip

Can you keep a secret?
Tu peux garder un secret?

🗣 too per garday er sekray

Do you have a boyfriend (a girlfriend)?
T'as un petit ami (une petite amie)?

🗣 tah er pteet amee (oon pteet amee)

An OK guy/An OK girl
Un mec sympa/Une fille sympa

🗣 er mek sampa/oon fee sampa

Way bossy!
Quel commandant!

🗣 kel comon–don

He/She's nutty!
Il/Elle est dingue!

🗣 eel/el ay dang

What a creep!
Quel râleur!

🗣 kel rah–ler

You won't make many friends saying this!

Bug off!
Dégage
👄 Day-gaj

Shut up!
La ferme!
👄 la ferm

If you're fed up with someone, and you want to say something like "you silly …!" or "you stupid …!", you can start with *"espèce de"* (which actually means "piece of …") and add anything you like. What about …

Stupid banana!
Espèce de banane!
(espes der banan)

or …

Silly sausage!
Espèce d'andouille!
(espes don-dooy)

Take your pick. It should do the trick. You could also try *"espèce d'idiot!"* *(espes dee-dyo)*. You don't need a translation here, do you?

Saying good-bye

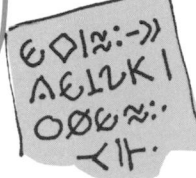

What's your address?
Tu m'donnes ton adresse?
👄 too mdon ton adres

Here's my address
Voilà mon adresse
👄 vla mon adres

Come to visit me
Viens chez moi
👄 vya shay mwa

Write to me soon
Écris-moi vite
👄 ekree mwa veet

Have a good trip!
Bon voyage!
👄 bon vwoy-arj

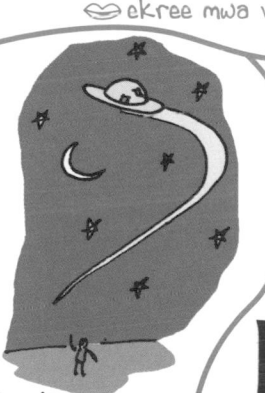

Bye!
Au revoir!
👄 oh rev-wa

Bone up on your French!
How do you say goodbye
to a skeleton?

Bone Voyage!

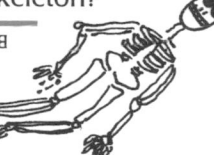

21

WANNA PLAY?

l'élastique
🗣 lelasteek

le ping-pong
🗣 ler "ping-pong"

la marelle
👄 la marel

la Gameboy®
👄 la "gameboy"

les billes
👄 les bee-yer

le yo-yó
👄 ler "yo yo"

Do you want to play ...?
Tu veux jouer ...?
👄 too ver joo-ay

... foos-ball?
... au baby-foot?
👄 oh baby foot

... cards?
... aux cartes?
👄 oh kart

... on the computer?
... sur l'ordinateur?
👄 syur lordee-nater

... tic-tac-toe?
... au morpion?
👄 oh more-pyon

... hide and seek?
... à cache-cache?
👄 a kash kash

... catch?
... au ballon?
👄 oh ballo

Not now.
Pas maintenant
👄 pah mat-non

Yeah!
Ouais!
👄 oo-way

Care for a game of **cat** or **leap sheep**?!

In France, playing tag is called playing "at cat"—*à chat* (*asha*). Whoever is "it" is the cat—*le chat* (*ler sha*). And you don't play "leap frog," you play "leap sheep"—*saute mouton* (*sote moo-ton*). Have you ever seen a sheep leaping? I ask you!

Make yourself heard

You're it!
Touché!
👄 tooshay

Who's winning?
Qui c'est qui gagne?
👄 kee say kee gan-yer

Race you!
On fait la course?
👄 on fay la koors?

I'm first
C'est moi le premier
👄 say mwa ler pre-myay

27

Electronic games

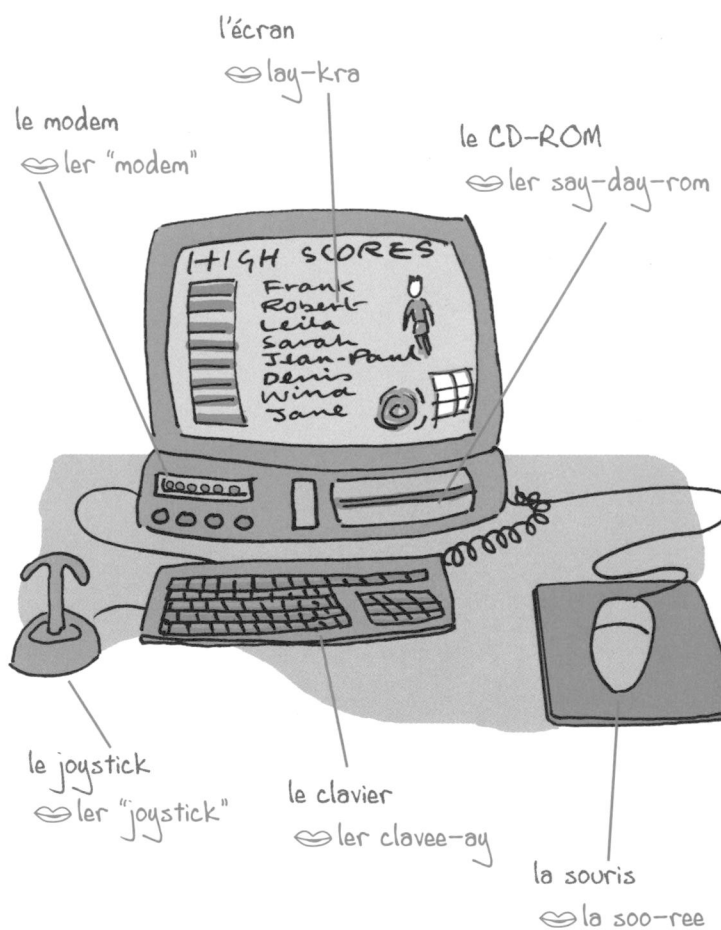

l'écran
~ lay-kra

le modem
~ ler "modem"

le CD-ROM
~ ler say-day-rom

le joystick
~ ler "joystick"

le clavier
~ ler clavee-ay

la souris
~ la soo-ree

HIGH SCORES

Frank
Robert
Leila
Sarah
Jean-Paul
Denis
Wina
Jane

What do I do?
Qu'est-ce que je fais?
💬 kesker jer fay

Show me
Montre-moi
💬 montrer mwa

Am I dead?
Ch'suis mort?
💬 shwee more

Shoot-em-up!
Tue-les!
💬 Tew lay

How many lives do I have?
J'ai combien de vies?
💬 jay konbee-yah der vee

How many levels are there?
Y'a combien de niveaux?
💬 yah konbee-yah de neevo

Non couch-potato activities!

tennis
le tennis
👄 ler "tennis"

trampolining
le trampoline
👄 ler "trampoline"

bowling
le bowling
👄 ler "bowling"

swimming
la natation
👄 la natasee-on

hockey
le hockey
👄 ler okee

gymnastics
la gymnastique
👄 la gymnasteek

ballet
le ballet
👄 ler ballay

basketball   le basket
👄 ler basket

and, of course, we haven't forgotten *"le foot"* ...

soccer

boots
les godasses
🗣 lay godas

shin-pads
les protèges
🗣 lay protej

ref
l'arbitre
🗣 lar–beetrer

soccer gear
les affaires de foot
🗣 layz afayr der foot

Well played!
Bien joué
🗣 beeyah joo–way

crossbar
la barre
🗣 la bar

goalpost
le poteau
🗣 ler potto

goal
le but
🗣 ler boo

goalie
le gardien
🗣 ler gardyen

Pass!
Passe!
🗣 pas

Offside!
Hors-jeu!
or-jer

You're on my team
T'es dans mon équipe
tay don mon ay-keep

Hands!
Y'a eu mains!
Ya ew man

Foul!
Coup-franc!
koo fron

Penalty!
Le penalty!
ler paynalty

He pushed me!
Il m'a poussé!
eel ma poo-say

Goal!
Goal!
just say it!

33

Keeping the others in line

Not like that!
Pas comme ça!
👄 pah kom sa

You cheat!
Tricheur! (boys only)/
Tricheuse! (girls only)
👄 tree-sher/
tree-sherz

I'm not playing anymore
Je joue plus
👄 jer joo ploo

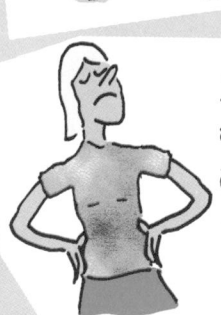

It's not fair!
C'est pas juste!
👄 say pah joost

Stop it!
Arrête!
👄 aret

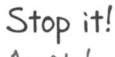

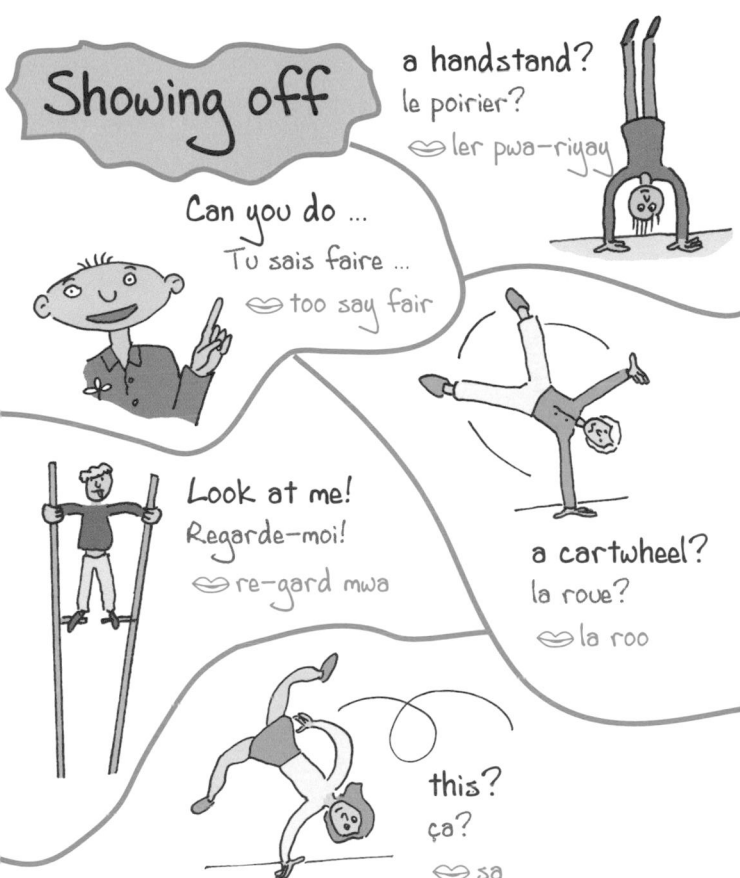

Impress your French friends with this!

You can show off to your new French friends by practicing this tongue twister:

Si ces six sausissons-ci sont six sous, ces six sausissons-ci sont très chers

see say see soseeson see son see soo, say see soseeson see son tray shair

(This means "If these six sausages cost six sous, these six sausages are very expensive.")

Then see if they can do as well with this English one:

"She sells sea shells on the sea shore, but the shells she sells aren't sea shells, I'm sure."

For a rainy day

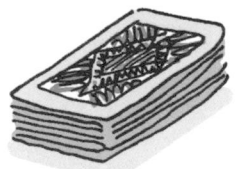 

pack of cards
un jeu de cartes
😮 er jer der kart

my deal/your deal
à moi la donne/à toi la donne
😮 a mwa la don/a twa la do

king
le roi
😮 ler rwa

queen
la dame
😮 la dam

jack
le valet
😮 ler valay

joker
le joker
😮 ler jokai

trèfle
😮 tray-fler

cœur
😮 kur

pique
😮 peek

carreau
😮 karo

Yes, the bishop's a fool in France!

chessboard
l'échiquier
☞ lay-sheek-yay

le fou
☞ ler foo

le cheval
☞ ler sherval

le pion
☞ ler pyon

la tour
☞ la toor

la reine
☞ la ren

le roi
☞ ler rwa

37

FEELING HUNGRY

hamburger
le steak haché
🖙 ler stek ashay

fries
les frites
🖙 lay freet

ice cream
la glace
🖙 la glas

coke
le coca
🖙 ler koka

38

snails

les escargots

🗣 layz eskargo

caramel custard

la crème caramel

🗣 la krem karamel

mussels

les moules

🗣 lay mool

orange juice

le jus d'orange

🗣 ler joo doronj

FEELING HUNGRY

Grub (la bouffe)

I'm starving
J'ai une faim de loup
 jay oon fam der loo

That means "I have the hunger of a wolf!"

le loup

Please can I have ...
Donnez-moi, s'il vous plaît ...
 donay mwa, seel voo play

... a chocolate pastry
un pain au chocolat
 er pan oh shokolah

... a croissant
un croissant
 er kruh-son

... an apple turnover
un chausson aux pommes
 er show-son oh pom

... a chocolate eclair
un éclair au chocolat
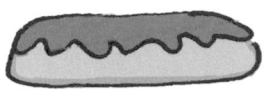
👄 un eklair oh shokolah

... a bun with raisins
un pain aux raisins
👄 er pan oh rayzan

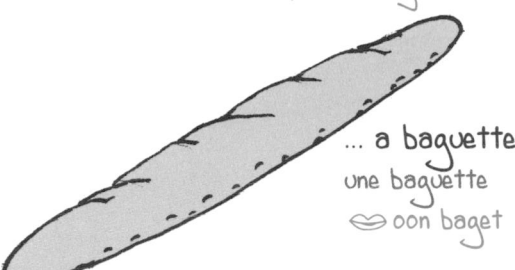
... a baguette
une baguette
👄 oon baget

... a pancake
une crêpe
👄 oon krep

... a waffle
une gaufre
👄 oon go-frer

Chocolate eclair? *"Miam, miam!"*
Snail pancake? *"Beurk!"*
If you're going to make food
noises, you'll need to know how
to do it properly in French!

"Yum, yum!" is out in French. You should
say *"Miam, miam!"* And "Yuk!" is
"Beurk" (pronounced "burk"), but
be careful not to let adults hear
you say this!

Drink up

I'm dying for a drink
Je meurs de soif
👄 jer mur der swaf

I'd like ...
Je voudrais ...
👄 jer voodray

... a coke
... un coca
👄 er koka

... an orange juice
... un jus d'orange
👄 er joo doronj

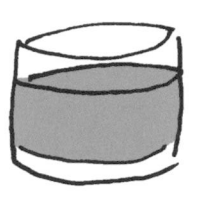

... an apple juice
... un jus de pommes
👄 er joo der pom

You can also have your lemon soda with flavored syrup—then it's called a "*diablo*." The most well-known is "*diablo de menthe*", lemonade with mint syrup—hmmm!

... a lemon soda
... une limonade
👄 oon leemonad

... a syrup
un sirop
👄 er seero

... a milkshake
... un milkshake
👄 er meelkshek

You get your hot chocolate in a bowl (and that, at least, is a decent amount).

... a hot chocolate
... un chocolat
👄 er shokolah

Did you know?

A lot of children have hot chocolate for breakfast in the morning and some of them will dip their croissants or bread in it. It gets very soggy and Mom is sure not to like this!

How did you like it?

That's lovely
C'est super-bon
👄 say soopair-bon

That's yummy
C'est géant
👄 say jay-on

I don't like that
J'aime pas ça
👄 jem pah sa

I'm stuffed
J'ai trop bouffé
👄 jay troh boofay

I can't eat that
Je mange pas ça
👄 jer monj pah sa

That's gross
C'est dégoutant
👄 say day-gooton

A "crunchy man" sandwich, please.

You never thought you could crunch up a man in France and get away with it, did you? Well, in France a grilled ham-and-cheese is:

un croque-monsieur
er krok murs-yur

… that means a "crunchy man." There's also a "crunchy woman!"

un croque-madame
er krok ma-dam

… which is the same but with a fried egg on top.

Tales of snails

Did you know that snails have to be put in a bucket of salt water for three days to clean out their insides (don't ask!) After that they are baked in the oven in their shells and eaten with tons of garlic butter. And many French kids still love them!

45

LOOKING GOOD

nail polish
le vernis à ongles
🔊 ler ver-nee a ong-ler

headband
le bandeau
🔊 ler band-o

bracelets
les bracelets
🔊 lay bracelay

braid
la natte
🔊 la nat

crop top
le débardeur
🔊 ler debad...

belt
la ceinture
🔊 la santee-your

miniskirt
la minijupe
🔊 la minee-joop

shoes
les chaussures
🔊 lay show-sur

bike
le vélo
🔊 ler vaylo

cap
la casquette
~ la kasket

le T-shirt
~ ler "T-shirt"

tattoo
le tatouage
~ ler tattoo-azh

le jean
~ ler jean

le walkman
~ ler "walkman"

le skateboard
~ ler "skateboard"

tennis shoes
les baskets
~ lay basket

LOOKING GOOD

47

That T-shirt, please
Ce T-shirt-là, s'il vous plaît
👄 ser "T-shirt" la, seel voo play

Cool tattoo!
Tatouage cool!
👄 tattoo-azh cool

The pink frilly one
Le rose à frous-frous
👄 ler roz a froo froo

A braid, please
Une natte, s'il vous plaît
👄 oon nat, seel voo play

The purple striped one
Le violet à rayure
👄 ler vee-oh-lau a rayure

Awesome miniskirt!
Minijupe d'enfer!
👄 minee-joop donfair

Where's my skateboard?
Où est mon skate-board?
👄 oo ay mon "skateboard"?

Where's my pant?!

The French don't wear "pant**s**" or "jean**s**," they wear only one of them: un pantalon *(ang pantaloh)*; un jean *(ang jeen)*. Strange, could've sworn they had two legs!

spotted
à pois
 a pwa

flowery
à fleurs
a fler

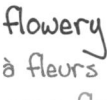

frilly
à frous-frous
a froo froo

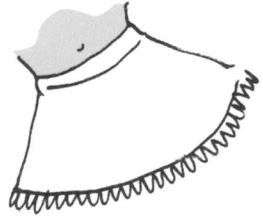

glittery
à paillettes
a pie-et

striped
à rayures
a rayure

jeans
le jean
👄 ler "jean"

T-shirt
le T-shirt
👄 ler "T-shirt"

sweatshirt
le sweat
👄 ler swet

tennis shoes
les baskets
👄 lay basket

dress
la robe
👄 la rob

skirt
la jupe
👄 la joop

pants
le pantalon
👄 ler panta-

soccer shirt
le maillot de foot
👄 ler mayo der foot

shorts
le short
👄 ler "short"

shoes
les chaussures
👄 lay show-s

50

Color this page yourself
(you can't expect us to do everything!)

colors
les couleurs
👄 lay coo-ler

white
blanc
👄 blon

green
vert
👄 vair

orange
orange
👄 oronzh

blue
bleu
👄 bler

pink
rose
👄 roz

yellow
jaune 👄 jone

red
rouge
👄 rooj

purple
violet
👄 vee-oh-lay

black
noir
👄 nwar

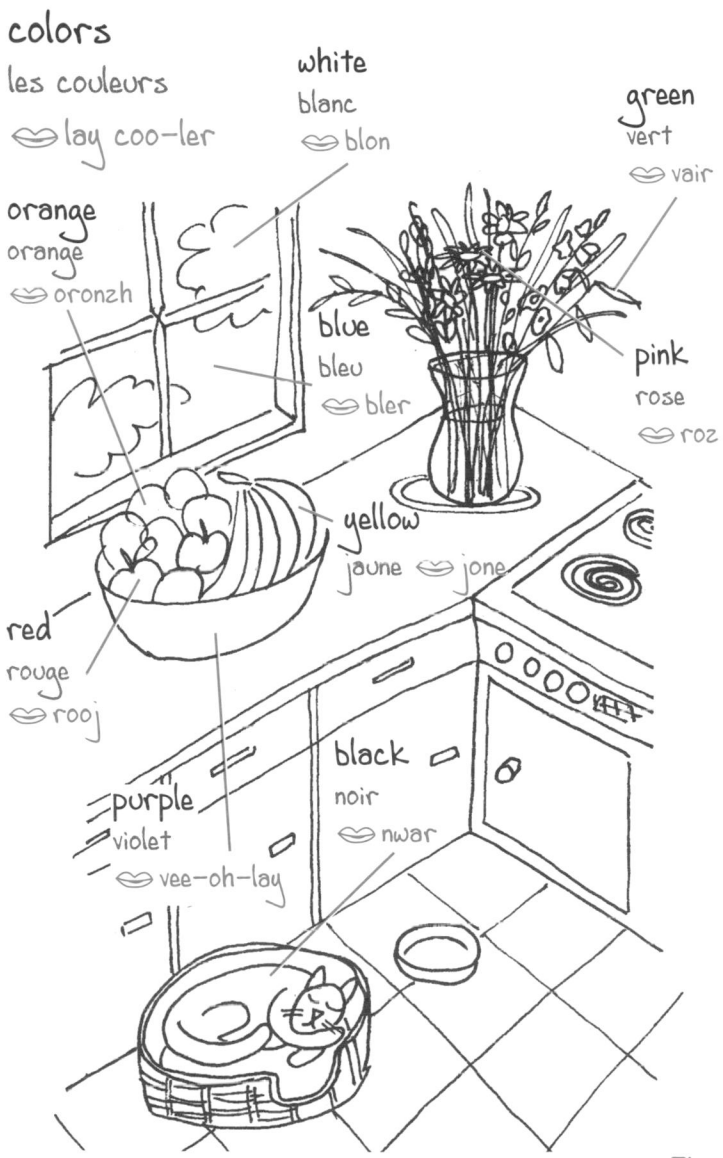

51

52

What should we do?
Qu'est-ce qu'on fait?
👄 kesk on fay

Can I come?
Je peux venir?
👄 jer per vuneer

Where do you all hang out?
Où trainez-vous?
👄 oo trainay voo

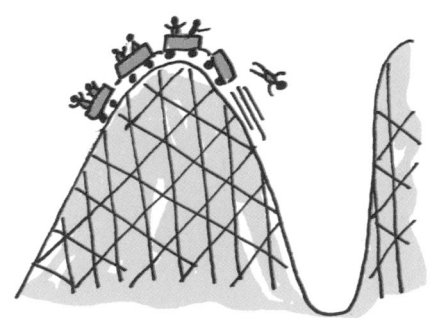

That's mega!
C'est géant!
👄 say jay-on

I'm (not) allowed
J'ai (pas) le droit
👄 jay (pa) ler drwa

Let's go back
On y retourne
👄 onny rutoorn

That gives me goose bumps (or "chicken flesh" in French!)
Ça m'donne la chair de poule
👄 sa mdon la shair der pool

I'm scared
J'ai la trouille
👄 jay la troo-yer

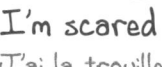

HOUSE OF MIRRORS

I'm bored to death
C'est mortel
👄 say mortell

That's funny
C'est marrant
👄 say maron

55

Beach babes

Can I borrow this?
Tu me prêtes ça?
≈ too mer pret sa

Let's hit the beach
On va à la plage
≈ on va a la plarzh

Is this your bucket?
C'est ton seau?
≈ say toh so

You can bury me
Tu peux m'enterrer
≈ too per moterray

Stop throwing sand!
Arrête de jeter du sable!
≈ arret der jetay dew sabler

Watch out for my eyes!
Attention à mes yeux!
≈ attensee-on a maiz yer

sea
la mer
la mair

beach
la plage
la plarj

sand castle
le château de sable
ler shato der sabler

towel
la serviette
la sir-vee-et

bathing suit
le maillot
ler my-yo

snorkel
e tuba
ler tew-ba

shells
les coquillages
lay kokeeyarj

bucket
le seau
ler so

spade
la pelle
la pel

How to get rid of your parents and eat lots of chocolate!

In France there are great beach clubs that organize all sorts of games as well as competitions (sand castles, sports, etc.). The prizes are often given by large companies who make kids' stuff such as chocolate and toys. Insist on signing up!

It's going swimmingly!

How to make a splash in French

PLOUF!

Let's hit the swimming pool
On va à la piscine
⇝ on va a la piseen

Can you swim (underwater)?
Tu sais nager (sous l'eau)?
⇝ too say najay (soo lo)

Me too/ I can't
Moi aussi/Moi pas
⇝ mwa os-see/ mwa pa

Can you dive?
Tu sais plonger?
⇝ too say plonjay

I'm getting changed
Je me change
⇝ jer mer shanzh

58

backstroke
le dos crawlé
👄 ler doe krolay

Can you do ...?
Tu sais faire ...?
👄 too say fair

butterfly
le papillon
👄 ler papeeyon

crawl
le crawl
👄 ler krol

breaststroke
la brasse
👄 la brass

slide
le toboggan
👄 ler tobogan

goggles
les lunettes de plongée
👄 lay loonet
der plonjay

Downtown

Do you know the way?
Tu connais le chemin?
too konay ler shema

Is it far?
C'est loin?
say lwan

Pooper-scoopers on wheels!

You might see bright green-and-white motorcycles with funny vacuum cleaners on the side riding around town scooping up the dog poop. The people riding the bikes look like astronauts! (Well, you'd want protection too, wouldn't you?)

Are we allowed in here?
On a le droit d'entrer ici?
on a ler drwa dentray eessee

Let's ask
On va demander
o va demonday

60

playground
l'aire de jeu
🗣 lair der jer

slide
le toboggan
🗣 ler tobogan

park
le parc
🗣 ler park

swings
la balançoire
🗣 la balonswar

bus
le bus
🗣 ler boos

car
la bagnole
🗣 la banyol

The "proper" French word for car is ***"voiture"*** (*vwat-yure*), but you'll look very uncool saying this. Stick to ***"bagnole"*** (*banyol*), or if the car is a wreck, try ***"tacot"*** (*taco*) for even more street cred: ***"Quel tacot!"*** (*kel tako*—"What an old clunker!").

61

Picnic (le pique-nique)

I hate wasps
Je déteste les guêpes
🗣 jer daytest
lay gep

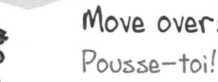

Move over!
Pousse-toi!
🗣 poos twa

bread
le pain
🗣 ler pan

Let's sit here
On s'assoie ici?
🗣 on saswa eess(

napkin
la serviette
🗣 la sir-vee-et

ham
le jambon
🗣 ler jambon

cheese
le fromage
🗣 ler fromarj

yogurt
le yaourt
🗣 ler ya-oort

chips
les chips
🗣 lay sheep

drinks
les boissons
👄 lay bwason

knife
le couteau
👄 ler koo-toe

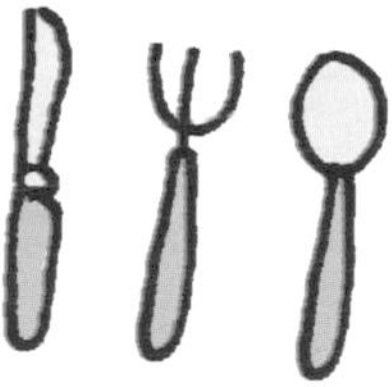

spoon
la cuillère
👄 la kwee-yeah

fork
la fourchette
👄 la four-shet

wasps
les guêpes
👄 lay gep

bees
les abeilles
👄 layz abay

bzzzz

ants
les fourmis
👄 lay foor-mee

All the fun of the fair

slide
le toboggan
〜 ler tobogan

Ferris wheel
la grande roue
〜 la grond roo

house of mirrors
le palais des glaces
〜 ler palay day glas

bumper cars
les autos tamponneuses
〜 layz oto tomponerz

Let's try this
On essaie ça?
〜 on essay sa

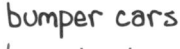

64

octopus
le manège
👄 ler manayj

It's (too) fast
Ca va (trop) vite
👄 sa va (tro) veet

That's for babies
C'est pour les petits
👄 say poor lay ptee

Do you get wet in here?
On sort mouillé d'ici?
👄 on sor moo-yay deessee

I'm not going on my own
J'y vais pas tout seul
👄 jee vay pa too surl

Spend it here

candy
les bonbons
👄 lay bonbon

les T-shirts
👄 lay "T-shirt"

toys
les jouets
👄 lay joo-ay

le vendeur
👄 ler von-d

books

les livres
 lay lee-vrer

le mobile
🗨 ler mobeel

les crayons
🗨 lay crayon
Watch out!
This means *pencils*
NOT crayons!

POCKET MONEY

What does that sign say?

Boucherie

boucherie
butcher shop
◡ booshree

pâtisserie
cake shop
◡ pateesree

boulangerie
bakery
◡ boolonjree

confiserie
candy store
◡ konfeesree

papeterie
office supplies
◡ paptree

épicerie
grocery stor...
◡ aypeesree

boutique de vêtements
clothes shop
◡ booteek der vetmon

Money talk

French money is **francs** (pronounced *fron*).
A franc is 100 **centimes** (*senteem*).
Coins: 5, 10, 20, 50 **centimes**

     1, 2, 5, 10, 20 **francs**

Notes: 20, 50, 100, 200, 500 **francs**
Make sure you know how much you are spending
before you blow all your pocket money at once!

Do you have some cash?
T'as des sous?
👄 tah day soo

I'm broke
Je suis fauché
👄 jer swee foshay

I'm loaded
J'ai plein d'sou
👄 jay pla dsoo

Here you go
Voilà
👄 vla

Can you lend me ten francs?
Tu peux me prêter dix franc
👄 too per mer pretay dee fron

No way!
Pas question!
👄 pa kes-tyo

That's a bargain
C'est pas cher
👄 say pa shair

It's a rip-off
C'est du vol
👄 say dew vol

Sweet heaven!

I love this shop
J'adore cette boutique
👄 jadore set booteek

Let's get some candy
On va acheter des bonbons
👄 on va ashtay day bonbon

Let's get some ice cream
On va acheter une glace
👄 on va ashtay oon glas

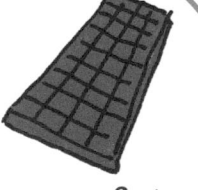

lollipops
des sucettes
👄 day sooset

a bar of chocolate
une tablette de chocolat
👄 oon tablet der shokola

chewing gum
chewing gum
👄 just say it, will you!

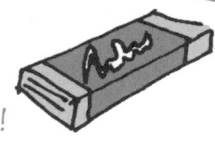

If you really want to look French and end up with lots of fillings, ask for:

des Carambars™
(day caram-bar)

medium-hard toffee-bars, now also available in all sorts of fruity flavors—also popular for the desperately silly jokes to be found inside the wrappings

des Malabars™ (day malabar)

bubble-gum, also popular for the tattoos provided with them

des nounours on chucolat
(day noonoor on shokola)

teddy-shaped marshmallow-type candy in chocolate coating

des frites (day freet)

fruity gums, slightly fizzy, shaped like fries

des Mini Berlingot™ (day mini berlingo)

sugary creamy stuff sold in small squishy packets—a bit like a small version of the "lunchbox" yogurts

des Dragibus™ (day drajibus)

multicolored licorice jelly beans

Other things you could buy

(that won't ruin your teeth!)

What are you getting?
Qu'est-ce tu prends?
👄 keska too pron

That toy, please
Ce jouet là, s'il vous plaît
👄 ser joo-ay la, seel voo play

Two postcards, please
Deux cartes postales,
s'il vous plaît
👄 der kart
post-tal,
seel voo play

How much is that?
C'est combien?
👄 say kombee-yah

This is garbage
C'est débile
👄 say daybeel

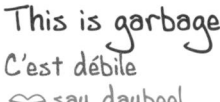

This is cool
C'est cool
👄 say kool

... colored pencils
des crayons de couleur
☞ day krayon der koolur

I'm getting ...
J'achète ... ☞ jashait

... stamps
des timbres
☞ day timbrer

... felt-tip pens
des feutres
☞ day fer-trer

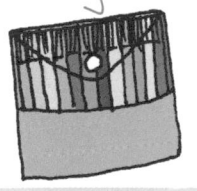

... a pen
un stylo
☞ er stee-lo

... a cassette
une cassette
☞ oon "cassette"

... a CD
un CD
☞ er say-day

... comics
des BD
☞ day bay day

For many years France's favorite comics have been Astérix and Tintin. They have both been translated into English, as well as into many other languages. Today children also like to read:

Tom Tom et Nana
Boule et Bill
Natacha
Gaston Lagaffe

GROWNUPTALK

It hurts here
J'ai mal ici
👄 jay mal eessee

bump
la bosse
👄 la bos

bandage
le sparadrap
👄 ler sparadra

child
enfant
👄 onfon

grown-up
adulte
👄 adoolt

Help!

Something has dropped/broken
Quelque chose est tombé/cassé
kel-ker shose ay tombay/kassay

Please
S'il vous plaît
seel voo play

Can you help me?
Vous pouvez m'aider?
voo poovay mayday

Where's the mailbox?
Où est la boîte aux lettres?
oo ay la bwat oh lettrer

Where are the toilets?
Où sont les toilettes?
oo son lay twalet

I can't manage it
Je n'y arrive pas
👄 jer nee arreev pah

Could you pass me that?
Vous pouvez me passer ça?
👄 Voo poovay mer passay sa

What time is it?
Quelle heure il est?
👄 kel ur eelay

Come and see
Venez voir
👄 venay vwar

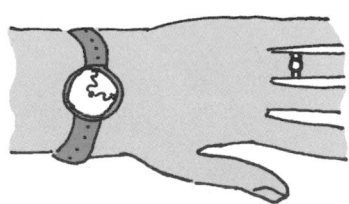

May I look at your watch?
Je peux voir sur votre montre?
👄 jer per vwar syur votrer montrer

Lost for words

... **my ticket**
mon billet
👄 mo beeyay

I've lost ...
J'ai perdu ...
👄 jay perdew

... **my bike**
mon vélo
👄 mo vaylo

... **my parents**
mes parents
👄 may paron

... **my shoes**
mes chaussures
👄 may sho-syur

... **my money**
mon argent
👄 mo arjon

... **my sweater**
mon pull
👄 mo pool

... **my watch**
ma montre
👄 ma montrer

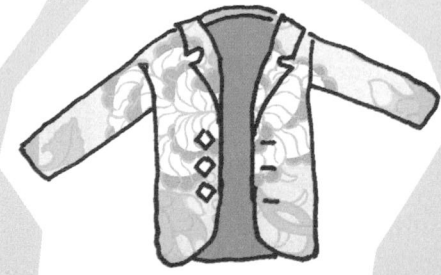

... **my jacket**
ma veste
👄 ma vest

ADULTS ONLY!

Show this page to adults who can't seem to make themselves clear (it happens). They will point to a phrase, you read what they mean, and you should all understand each other perfectly.

Ne t'en fais pas
Don't worry

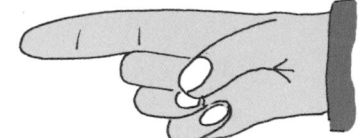

Assieds-toi ici
Sit down here

Quel est ton nom et ton prénom?
What's your name and surname?

Quel âge as-tu?
How old are you?

D'où viens-tu?
Where are you from?

Où habites-tu?
Where are you staying?

Où est-ce que tu as mal?
Where does it hurt?

Est-ce que tu es allergique à quelque chose?
Are you allergic to anything?

C'est interdit
It's forbidden

Tu dois être accompagné d'un adulte
You have to have an adult with you

Je vais chercher quelqu'un qui parle anglais
I'll get someone who speaks English

There was an English cat called "one, two, three" and a French cat called "un, deux, trois" standing waiting to cross a river. Both were afraid of water, so the English cat suggested that they race across to make it more fun. Who won?

Answer: "One, two, three" because "un, deux, trois" CAT SANK!

un   👄 un

deux   👄 der

trois   👄 twa

quatre   👄 katrer

cinq   👄 sank

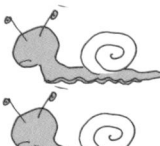

six	👄 sees	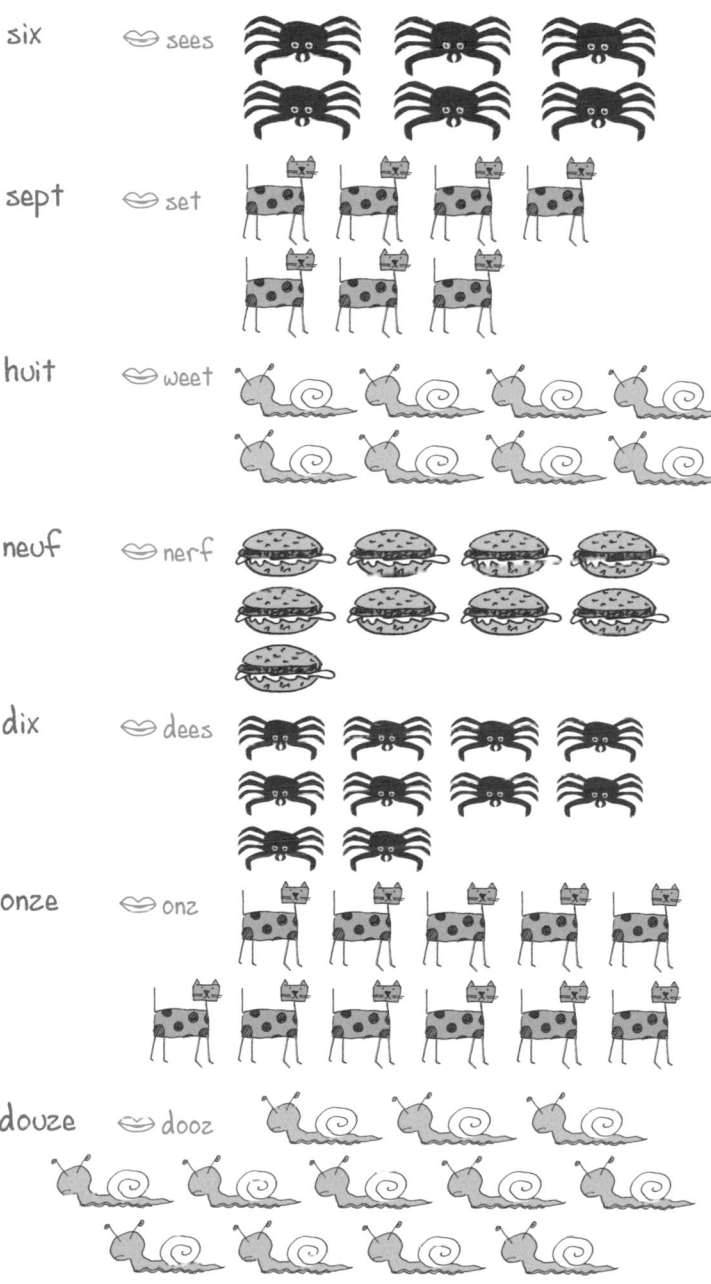
sept	👄 set	
huit	👄 weet	
neuf	👄 nerf	
dix	👄 dees	
onze	👄 onz	
douze	👄 dooz	

13	treize	*trez*	17	dix-sept	*dees-set*
14	quatorze	*catorz*	18	dix-huit	*dees-weet*
15	quinze	*kanz*	19	dix-neuf	*dees-nerf*
16	seize	*sez*	20	vingt	*van*

If you want to say "twenty-two," "sixty-five," and so on, you can just put the two numbers together like you do in English:

22 **vingt-deux** *van der*

65 **soixante cinq** *swasont sank*

This works except if you're saying "twenty-one," "sixty-one," and so on. Then you need to add the word for "and" (**et**) in the middle:

21 **vingt et un** *vant eh un*

61 **soixante et un** *swasont eh un*

30	trente	*tront*
40	quarante	*karont*
50	cinquante	*sankont*
60	soixante	*swasont*
70	soixante-dix	*swasont dees*
80	quatre-vingts	*katrer van*
90	quatre-vingt-dix	*katrer van dees*
100	cent	*sonn*

The French must be really big on sums! Everything's fine until you reach 70. Instead of saying "seventy," they say "sixty-ten" (**soixante-dix**) and keep counting like this until they reach 80. So 72 is "sixty-twelve" (**soixante douze**), 78 is "sixty-eighteen" (**soixante dix-huit**), and so on.

Just so it doesn't get too easy, for 80 they say "4 twenties!" And to really make your brain ache they continue counting like this until a hundred. So 90 is "4 twenties 10" (**quatre-vingt-dix**), 95 is "4 twenties fifteen" (**quatre-vingt-quinze**) … you have remembered your calculator, haven't you??

March	mars	*mars*
April	avril	*avreel*
May	mai	*meh*

June	juin	*joo-wah*
July	juillet	*joowee-eh*
August	août	*oot*

September	septembre	*septombrer*
October	octobre	*octobrer*
November	novembre	*novombrer*

December	décembre	*desombrer*
January	janvier	*jonvee-eh*
February	février	*fevree-eh*

87

printemps *prantom*

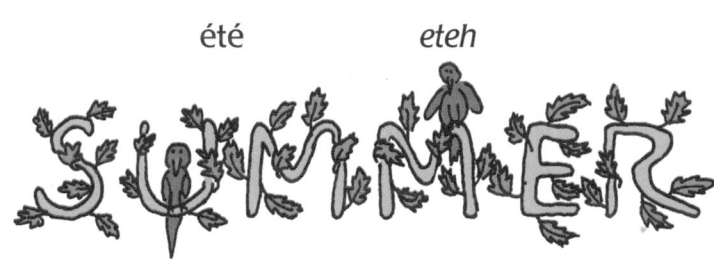
SPRING

été *eteh*

SUMMER

automne *awtom*

FALL

hiver *eever*

WINTER

Monday	lundi	*lundee*
Tuesday	mardi	*mardee*
Wednesday	mercredi	*mecredee*
Thursday	jeudi	*jurdee*
Friday	vendredi	*vendredee*
Saturday	samedi	*samdee*
Sunday	dimanche	*deemonsh*

By the way, French kids don't usually have school on Wednesdays, but they have to go on Saturday mornings. Still—that's half a day less than you!

Good times

It's ...
Il est ...
👄 eel ay

(one) o'clock
(une) heure
👄 (oon) ur

quarter after (two)
(deux heures) et quart
👄 (der zur) ay kar

quarter to (four)
(quatre heures) moins le quart
👄 (katr ur) mwan ler kar

half past (three)
(trois heures) et demie
👄 (twa zur) ay demee

five after (ten)
(dix heures) cinq
👄 dees ur sank

twenty after (eleven)
(onze heures) vingt
👄 onz ur van

ten to (four)
(quatre heures) moins dix
👄 (katr ur) mwan dees

twenty to (six)
(six heures) moins vingt
👄 (sees ur) mwan van

morning
matin
 ma-tah

midday
midi
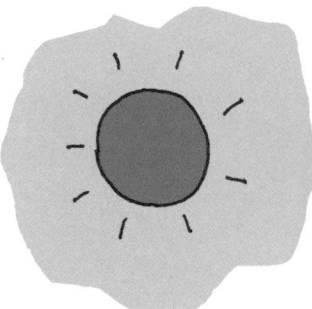 meedee

afternoon
après-midi
 apray meedee

midnight
minuit
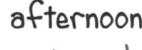 meenwee

evening
soir
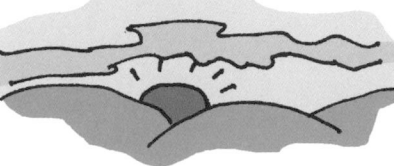 swar

Weather wise

Can we go out?
On peut sortir?
👄 on per sorteer

It's hot
Il fait chaud
👄 eel fay show

It's cold
Il fait froid
👄 eel fay frwa

It's horrible
Il fait mauvais
👄 eel fay movay

It's raining ropes!

In French it doesn't rain "cats and dogs," it rains "ropes!" That's what they say when it's raining really heavily:

Il pleut des cordes
eel pler day kord

It's windy
Il fait du vent
👄 eel fay dew von

It's sunny
Il fait du soleil
👄 eel fay dew solay

It's snowing
Il neige
👄 eel nej

It's raining
Il pleut
👄 eel pler

I'm soaked
Je me suis fait tremper
👄 jer muswee fay trompay

It's nice
Il fait beau
👄 eel fay bow

Cheat Sheet

No
Non
🗨 non

Yes
Oui 🗨 wee

Hi!
Salut!
🗨 saloo

Thanks
Merci 🗨 mer-see

Where?
Où?
🗨 oo

How much? Combien?
🗨 kombee-yah

Please
(to grown-ups)
S'il vous plaît
🗨 seel voo play

(to children)
S'il te plaît
🗨 seel ter play

Bye! au revoir
🗨 oh rev-wa